STEREOGRAM

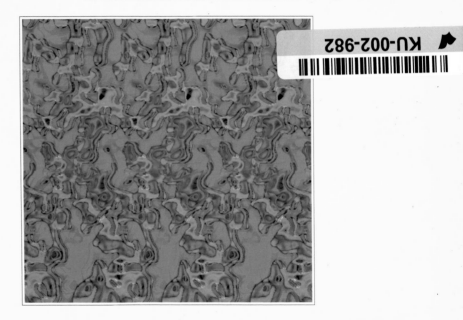

KU-002-982

P O S T C A R D   C O L L E C T I O N

BOXTREE

Executive Editor/Seiji Horibuchi
Publisher/Masahiro Oga

© Cadence Books, 1994

All rights reserved.
No images or text from this volume
may be reproduced without the
express written permission
of the publisher.

Printed in Japan

ISBN 0-7522-0890-X

10 9 8 7 6 5 4 3 2 1

First published in the UK 1994 by
Boxtree Limited
21 Broadwall
London SEI 9PL

Cover Artwork/
Tetrahedral Star by Shiro Nakayama
Back Cover Artwork/
Silent Beauties 91.3 by Naoyuki Kato
Title Page Artwork/Untitled by DIN

"Stereogram" is the generic term for two-dimensional images which, when viewed in the right way, appear to be three-dimensional. Each work presented here contains a three-dimensional image that can be seen with the naked eye.

There are two ways to see a stereogram. Each image is intended to be seen one of two ways, parallel or cross-eyed. Be sure to use the appropriate technique for best results.

THE PARALLEL TECHNIQUE
This technique involves making the lines of sight of the left and right eyes nearly parallel, as if looking at something far away. Without losing that focal point, hold the image flat up against your face. Move the image ever so slowly away from your face. The image will be blurry at first, but that's okay. Your eyes will gradually find the stereogram's focus point on their own.

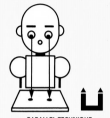

PARALLEL TECHNIQUE

THE CROSS-EYED TECHNIQUE
This technique involves crossing your eyes so that the lines of sight of the left and right eyes intersect. Hold up your finger or a similar object (such as a pen) between your eyes and the image. Look at the tip of the object. Maintaining your focus, gradually adjust the difference between the object and the image. When the correct position is reached, the 3-D image should come into view.

CROSS-EYED TECHNIQUE

How to "See" a Stereogram

Each image in this postcard collection is marked with a symbol indicating which method, parallel or cross-eyed, should be used to view that work.

Pegasus
Shiro Nakayama

*Bellerophon's winged horse in
a rainbow-colored sky.*

STEREOGRAM POSTCARD COLLECTION
© Cadence Books, 1994

Heart
Shiro Nakayama
A bouquet with heart.

STEREOGRAM POSTCARD COLLECTION
© Cadence Books, 1994

Aster
Shiro Nakayama

*Try both the parallel and
cross-eyed techniques.*

ⱢⅩ

STEREOGRAM POSTCARD COLLECTION
© Cadence Books, 1994

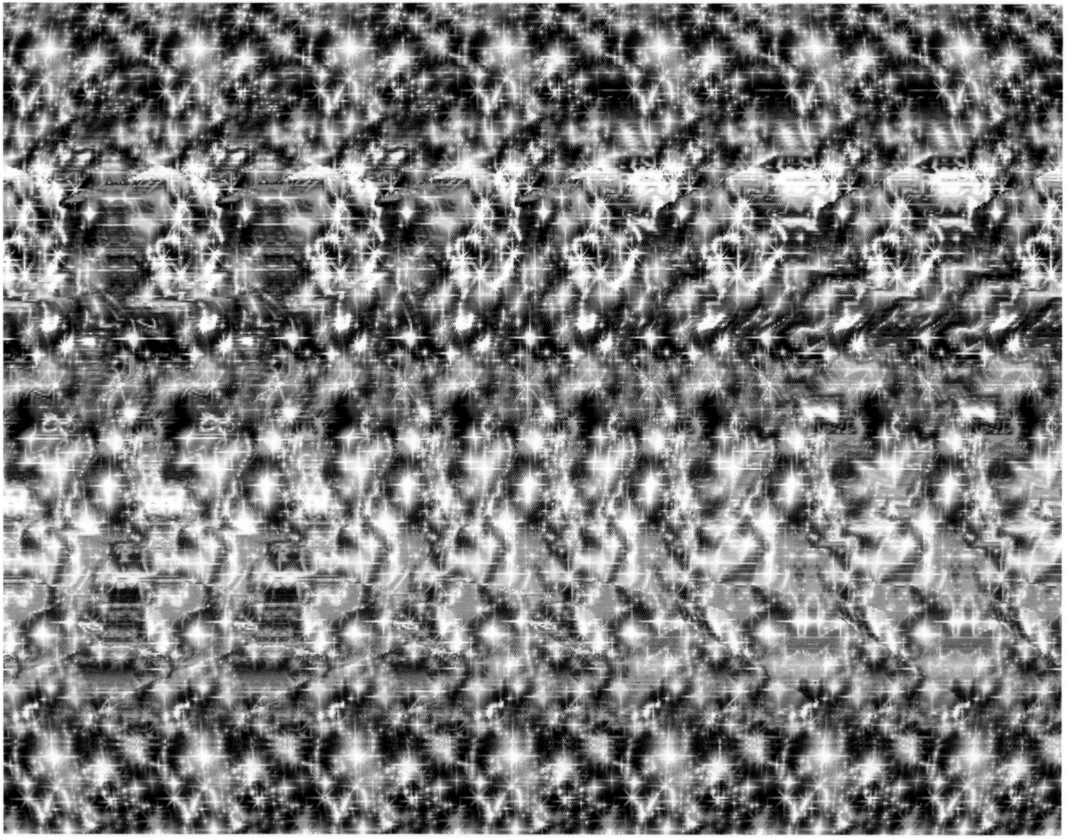

Tetrahedral Star
Shiro Nakayama

A five-pointed star in the
center of a ten-pointed star.

STEREOGRAM POSTCARD COLLECTION
© Cadence Books, 1994

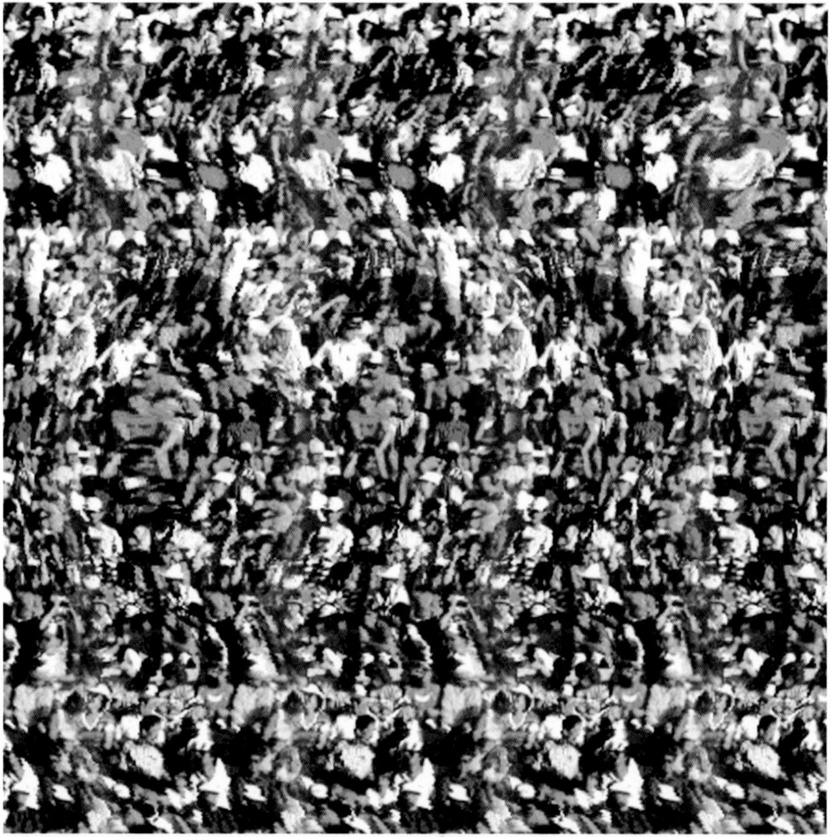

Untitled
DIN

*A crowd becomes a
living color field.*

LIX

STEREOGRAM POSTCARD COLLECTION
© Cadence Books, 1994

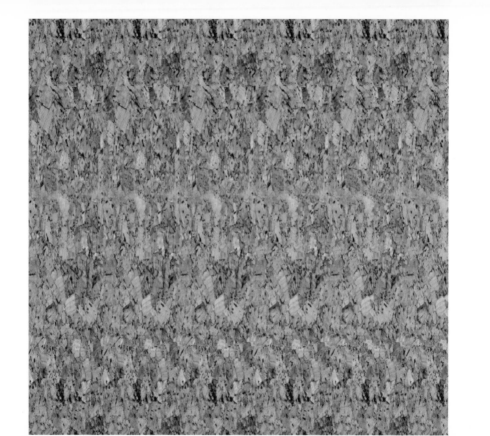

Mimesis
Michiru Minagawa

Natural mimesis is a reversal
of the stereogram effect.

STEREOGRAM POSTCARD COLLECTION
© Cadence Books, 1994

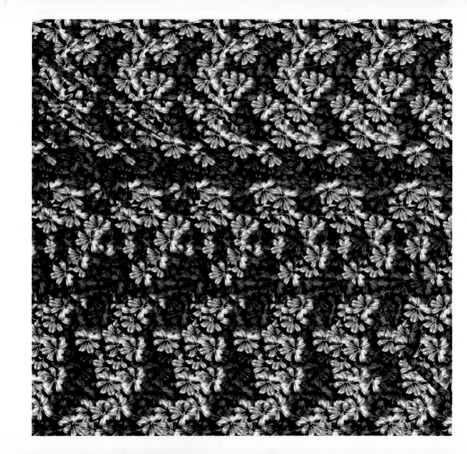

Sniper
Michiru Minagawa
*Something hidden is
aiming right at you.*

STEREOGRAM POSTCARD COLLECTION
© Cadence Books, 1994

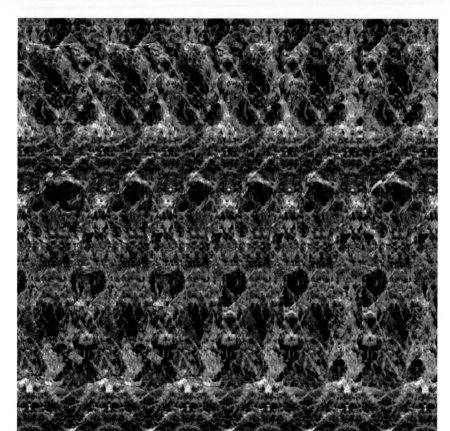

Skeleton
Eiji Takaoki

The exquisite marble background
fits this 3-D image perfectly.

STEREOGRAM POSTCARD COLLECTION
© Cadence Books, 1994

Jungle
Takashi Taniai

*Spot the stegosaurus
in this primeval forest.*

STEREOGRAM POSTCARD COLLECTION
© Cadence Books, 1994

Twilight in Paradise
Takashi Taniai

These sauropods may know
the fate of their species.

STEREOGRAM POSTCARD COLLECTION
© Cadence Books, 1994

The Forest Comes to Life
Hiroshi Kunoh
What is flying in the trees?

STEREOGRAM POSTCARD COLLECTION
© Cadence Books, 1994

In the Wrong Body of Water
Hiroshi Kunoh

There's something...well, unnatural, in this nature photograph.

STEREOGRAM POSTCARD COLLECTION
© Cadence Books, 1994

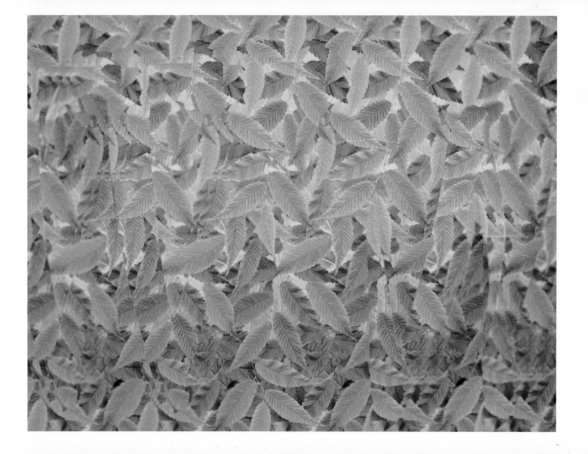

Hunter
Hiroshi Kunoh

*The small predator in the leaves
is about to attack its prey.*

STEREOGRAM POSTCARD COLLECTION
© Cadence Books, 1994

Christmas
Hiroshi Kunoh

*Christmas lights are brighter
this year in 3-D.*

STEREOGRAM POSTCARD COLLECTION
© Cadence Books, 1994

Landscape
Miyuki Kato
Inspired by illustrator Maxfield Parrish.

STEREOGRAM POSTCARD COLLECTION
© Cadence Books, 1994

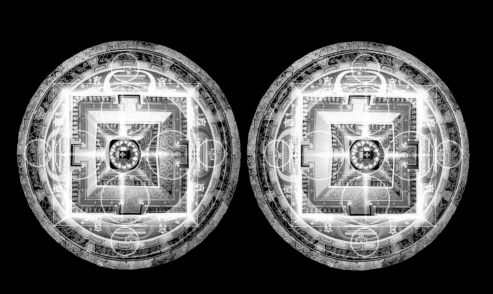

Mandala
Makoto Sugiyama
*A 3-D interpretation of a
Buddhist art form.*

STEREOGRAM POSTCARD COLLECTION
© Cadence Books, 1994

Wa no Yumeji
(The Circle's Dream World)
Mayumi Dava

In the center is a visual play on the
Japanese word for "dream."

STEREOGRAM POSTCARD COLLECTION
© Cadence Books, 1994

Ishigaki (Stone Wall)
Jun Oi

*A meticulously crafted
photo-field stereogram.*

STEREOGRAM POSTCARD COLLECTION
© Cadence Books, 1994

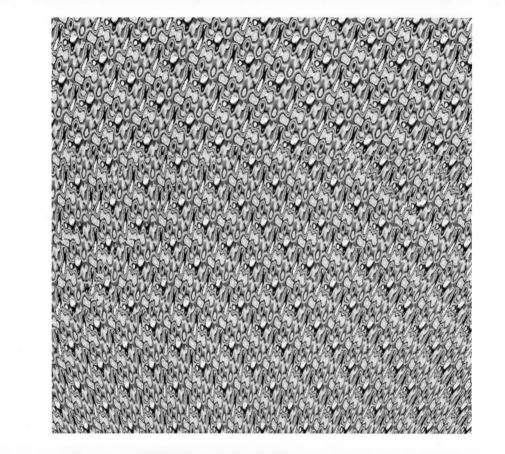

Beetle
Izuru Fujita

The classic Volkswagen
parked on an incline.

STEREOGRAM POSTCARD COLLECTION
© Cadence Books, 1994

Silent Beauties 91.3
Naoyuki Kato
Is their silence golden?

STEREOGRAM POSTCARD COLLECTION
© Cadence Books, 1994

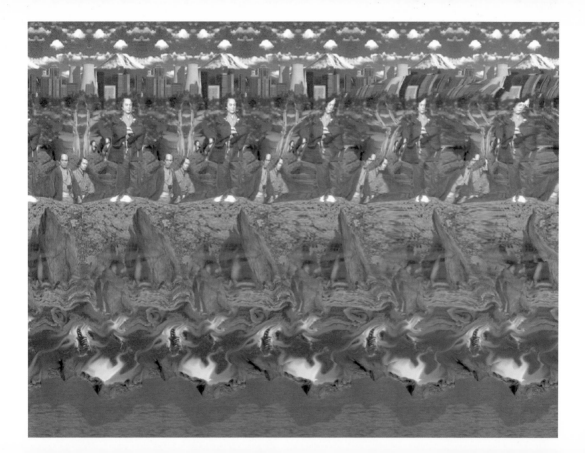

Time Trap
DIN

*Japan's past and present
mixed in 3-D.*

STEREOGRAM POSTCARD COLLECTION
© Cadence Books, 1994

Not Really
DIN

*Japanese businessmen's
dilemma, according to DIN.*

STEREOGRAM POSTCARD COLLECTION
© Cadence Books, 1994